GEORGIA O'KEEFFE

Painter of the Desert

by
Jacqueline A. Ball
and
Catherine Conant

A BLACKBIRCH PRESS™ BOOK

THE ROSEN PUBLISHING GROUP, INC.

Published by Blackbirch Press™ in conjunction with The Rosen
Publishing Group, Inc., 29 East 21st Street, New York, NY 10010

©1991 Blackbirch Press™ a division of Blackbirch Graphics, Inc.
First Edition

Printed in Hong Kong
Bound in the United States of America

Editors: Kailyard Associates
Art Director: Cynthia Minichino

Photo Research by Photosearch, Inc.

Library of Congress Cataloging-in-Publication Data

Ball, Jacqueline A.,
    Georgia O'Keeffe/Jacqueline A. Ball.
    (The Library of famous women)
    "A Blackbirch Press book."
    Includes bibliographical references.
    Includes index.
    Summary: Examines the life and works of the painter who drew
much of her artistic inspiration from nature.
    ISBN 0-8239-1207-8
    1. O'Keeffe, Georgia, 1887–1988 —Juvenile literature. 2. Artists—
United States—Biography—Juvenile literature. [1. O'Keeffe, Georgia,
1887–1986. 2. Artists. 3. Painting, American. 4. Art appreciation.]
I. Title. II. Series.
N6537.039B35 1990
759.13—dc20
[B]
[92]   90-47348
                                                   CIP
                                                    AC

Contents

Chapter 1

Patterns in the Prairie

Georgia O'Keeffe was a modern American artist. She was most famous for spectacular, larger-than-life paintings of objects from nature: flowers, shells, bones. The way she lived was larger than life, too. At a time when women's lives were limited and confined, her life was as free and limitless as the vast, open landscape into which she was born.

Georgia was born in Sun Prairie, Wisconsin, on November 15, 1887. Her parents, Frank O'Keeffe and Ida Totto O'Keeffe, already had a toddler, Francis. In time they would have five more children, four girls and another boy. The O'Keeffes were a farming family. By Midwest farm standards, seven children wasn't very large. Farms needed lots of children to help with the work. Georgia grew up happy and free-spirited in the busy O'Keeffe household.

Her parents were very different from each other. Georgia remembered her father, Frank, as "very jolly," someone always ready for excitement and travel. He also had strong ties to nature and the earth.

Georgia's mother, Ida, was more reserved. She was devoted to education and read whenever she could. Often she would read aloud to her children—books like *The Last of the Mohicans* and *The Adventures of Kit Carson*. She could also play any music she heard on the piano.

Both Georgia's parents were hard working and encouraged independence. Though they were not wealthy, they were good farmers with good land. They managed their money carefully to give their children a comfortable, secure life.

From the beginning, Georgia was aware of the shapes, colors, and patterns around her. She remembers as an infant dazzling bright sunlight and red, white, and black patterns. She had been brought outside and placed on a quilt. The quilt pattern was red stars and red and white flowers on black and white backgrounds.

On the farm, nature was all around her. She found beauty everywhere she looked. "I remember the beautiful fields of grain and wheat out there—like snow—only

Ida Totto O'Keeffe, Georgia's mother.

yellow…in spring," she said later. "They were plowing, and there were patterns of plowed ground and patches where things were growing."

Georgia's strong visual sense was matched by a strong streak of stubbornness and independence. She was always her own person. She did what she wanted. And she made other people do things her way, too—especially her sisters, Catherine, Anita, Claudia, and young Ida, named after her mother. She was nice to them, and they loved her. But she bossed them around constantly. Georgia's sister Catherine said she acted like "a queen." Georgia herself said later, "I had a sense of power."

Some of that power came naturally because she was the oldest sister. This gave her authority — one reason why her sisters let her boss them around and why they accepted her having her own room while they had to share. But the other reason was she was just special.

Georgia took her uniqueness and the privileges that she received for granted. She knew she was different, and she enjoyed acting that way. She rebelled against being like anyone else. Other girls wore fancy dresses, but Georgia wore plain ones. When other girls tied ribbons in their hair,

Georgia let her dark locks fall straight and untrimmed. This plain, unfussy look, which was best for her strong, dark features, would become her trademark.

Frank O'Keeffe, Georgia's father.

An Independent Child

On Sundays, Georgia drove the horse and buggy to church, taking the reins as easily as she took control of everything else. She did things other people wouldn't think of doing.

Georgia's independent thinking meant she spent a lot of time alone. She didn't mind a bit. She had her imagination for company, and she imagined a world of her own making.

When she was very young, her dolls and dollhouse made up a large part of Georgia's world. The dollhouse was really two thin boards slit halfway down so they fit together like a cross. But in her mind, the cross became the inner walls of four rooms. Inside these rooms she could make her dolls behave any way she wished.

Georgia would take the dollhouse outside and create a miniature country estate. She clipped patches of grass with scissors to look like a lawn. She filled a dishpan with water and called it a lake.

Georgia, in 1893, age 6.

Georgia's pockets were always filled with scraps of material so she could whip up new doll clothes in a moment. All the O'Keeffe girls were taught to sew when they were very small. Georgia was particularly good at it.

Georgia loved her fantasy world. She spent as much time as she could in it. But real life on the farm was fun, too. In between chores such as cooking, sewing, and hoeing and weeding the huge vegetable garden, there were games to play and two big swings behind the barn.

Of course, most of the time the children went to school. Georgia wasn't much of a student. She said later, "My memories of childhood are quite pleasant, although I hated school." For the O'Keeffe children, there was not only regular school but extra lessons in drawing and music.

The lessons were Ida O'Keeffe's idea. Georgia's mother loved learning so much that she herself had once wanted to become a doctor. Marriage, family, and farm life ended that dream. But Ida was determined her children would have as much education as she could afford. Writing, reading, and arithmetic weren't enough. Ida wanted them to study the fine arts, too.

She knew that couldn't happen in the one-room schoolhouse they attended. So she arranged private music and drawing lessons.

Georgia approached drawing lessons like she approached everything else: intensely. She concentrated hard. She tried hard. She never gave up. Later, she remembered trying to draw a man bending over. She tried and tried but couldn't make his knees bend the right way. He looked like he was about to fall over.

Finally, she found a solution. By turning the paper around so the man lay on his back with his legs in the air, he looked much more natural. Even at this early age, Georgia O'Keeffe was not afraid to try an unusual approach.

Colors and Questions

Georgia and her sisters became more skilled at drawing, but soon that wasn't enough for Ida. She wanted them to learn to paint. One Saturday a month they made a seven-mile buggy trip to study with Mrs. Sarah Mann.

Mrs. Mann taught art by imitation. Students picked illustrations from books and copied them in watercolor. Obediently, Georgia copied pictures of flowers and Arabian horses. But she was never satisfied with the results. What she painted just didn't look enough like the originals.

Soon she wasn't satisfied with copying at all. She was doing her own paintings at home. She began to experiment with color. How could she paint snow to look the way it did in moonlight? Maybe by leaving the paper blank? How could she make trees look as black as they did through her window at midnight? Maybe by mixing a little dark blue with black.

She was searching for her own, personal art direction. It was a search that would occupy her whole life.

Her family noticed Georgia's talent. Her mother was delighted. Maybe Georgia would become an art teacher. Of course, being a real artist was out of the question. Girls simply didn't lead the unconventional, shockingly free-spirited life of a practicing artist.

But Georgia had already shown she wasn't typical. In eighth grade she made it clearer. She told her friend Lena: "I'm going to be an artist."

"I'm going to be an artist"

Chapter 2

Beyond the Prairie

In 1901, when she was 14, Georgia entered a private Catholic school in Madison, Wisconsin. Her parents paid extra money so she could take art. The art teacher, Sister Angelique, was good and very demanding.

Georgia, age 16, in 1903.

For her first assignment, Georgia worked hard on a charcoal drawing. She made a picture of a baby's hand and brought it to Sister Angelique. Georgia felt sure it was good. But she was shocked and embarrassed when the nun told her it was too small and messy. Sister Angelique showed Georgia how a better picture could be made using large, light lines instead of small, dark ones.

Georgia promised herself she would never draw little pictures again. For the rest of the term she worked on her drawings. By the end of the school year the classroom walls were covered with them. She was the best art student.

The following year, 1902, brought many changes. Ida O'Keeffe sent Georgia and her older brother Francis to high school in Milwaukee. They lived with Ida's sister, Lola. Both children loved living in the big city, and they often went exploring.

Georgia wasn't too excited about school. She was disappointed with the art teacher, a thin, nervous woman who wore a straw hat decorated with violets. Then one day the teacher brought a Jack-in-the-Pulpit flower to class. She told the students to use it as a drawing model.

Georgia was astonished to realize that she could draw pictures of everyday objects. Looking around her, she saw an endless number of things to draw. Suddenly, Georgia looked at things more closely.

She began to draw more details in her pictures. Sometimes she drew only a part of a flower, concentrating on the curves of a leaf or petal. "When you take a flower in your hand and really look at it, it's your world for the moment," she would say later.

"When you take a flower in your hand and really look at it, it's your world for the moment"

A New Home

While Francis and Georgia were at school in Milwaukee, their parents decided to move the family away from Sun Prairie. As much as they loved the farm, it was hard work for everyone. The winter months in Wisconsin were long and cold, with bitter winds and fierce snowstorms. And there was a family history of tuberculosis. Maybe by moving to a warmer place they could all stay healthy. Frank and Ida sold the farm and bought a house and general store in Williamsburg, Virginia.

Life in Williamsburg was very different from life on the prairie. Instead of open plains and fields, there were gentle rolling hills. The warmer weather and colorful flowering trees made everyone feel like they had moved into a beautiful garden.

Georgia often hiked deep into the woods by herself. She liked to disappear into the forest to observe the colors and shapes of the natural world.

In 1903, Georgia started at the Chatham Episcopal Institute. It was a small school deep in the Blue Ridge Mountains of Virginia. Chatham was a private school.

Georgia wasn't like the rest of the girls in her class. Her dresses were still dark and plain. She still wore no frills or ribbons in her hair.

Even though she was different, her fun-loving personality made her popular. She

Georgia entered a private Catholic school in Madison, Wisconsin when she was fourteen. Madison was a big, exciting city compared to her hometown.

was always ready to play a trick or do something daring and unconventional: take a walk alone (which wasn't allowed), or teach her classmates how to play poker. The same strong-willed, independent little girl who had driven the buggy to church was now older, but not any tamer.

Georgia's unusual artistic talent also made her stand out at Chatham. Her abilities were quickly noticed by both teachers and students. She was allowed to use the art room all the time. She made the room her personal studio. Soon the walls were covered with her work.

Classmates would often beg for the pictures that she had drawn, but Georgia always refused. "I don't want any of them floating around to haunt me later," she would say.

Georgia did very well in art and very poorly in her other subjects. In fact, she almost didn't graduate because of a spelling test. She needed to get at least 75 out of 100 words right. Finally, on the sixth try, she spelled 76 words right.

At graduation in 1905, the girls all said goodbye. Most of them expected to return home and be married within a few years. But Georgia told her friends, "I am going to give up everything for my art."

Chapter 3

City Scenes and Still Lifes

Georgia's parents agreed she should have more art training after Chatham. They picked the Art Institute of Chicago. Ida's sister Ollie and brother Charles lived within walking distance of the school. Georgia could stay with them.

A portrait of eighteen-year-old Georgia, painted by a classmate at the Art Students League in New York.

Seventeen-year-old Georgia made the long train trip to Chicago from Virginia in September of 1905. She said she felt "a special kind of sick." She had good reason to be nervous. Chatham had been small and friendly. What would this big school be like?

At least Aunt Ollie would be around. Like her sister Ida, Ollie was full of determination. But Ollie had gone way beyond her sister, and just about every woman of her time. Ollie had run a business. Presently she was the only woman in a newspaper office. She was a strong role model for Georgia, her favorite niece.

William Meritt Chase taught Georgia portrait painting.

As nice as it was to be with Aunt Ollie, Georgia's first impressions of the Art Institute weren't so great. Everything about it was huge. The classrooms were as big as basketball courts.

Georgia soon found that the classes weren't too inspiring, either. There wasn't much chance to use color, which Georgia loved. And students spent most of their time copying the great European artists.

The place was also extremely competitive. Students were judged every week on their work. Those who got good reports could move their easels closer to the front of the huge studio rooms. That way they were allowed better and better views of what they were painting. Poorer students kept moving further back.

Georgia moved forward—fast. By January she ranked first in the class. Although she was successful, she had one big problem. She absolutely dreaded her anatomy classes. These classes taught students how to draw the human body. They used young men as models—young men who were practically naked.

Even though her classmates were all girls, Georgia found the whole thing terribly embarrassing. But anatomy was required, so she had no choice. She made herself get through it. Later, though, and throughout her career, she rarely painted people. She chose objects from nature instead.

Georgia expected to return to the Art Institute after summer vacation, but she never did. She came down with a serious illness called typhoid fever. By the time she recovered, school had already begun. She stayed in Williamsburg a year, painting a little and getting back her strength.

By the fall of 1907, she was back on her feet. Her art teacher from Chatham, Mrs. Elizabeth May Willis, urged her to go to the Art Students League in New York. The general store wasn't doing too well. But Ida O'Keeffe was just as determined as ever. They found the money somewhere, and Georgia set out for New York City.

New York buzzed with newness and excitement. It was quickly changing into a modern twentieth-century city. Elevated trains, trolleys, and subways were replacing the old horse-drawn buses. Tall office buildings called "skyscrapers" were just beginning to be built as businesses boomed.

Georgia dove right into the excitement. She found a room at a boarding house and settled into her art classes. She was quickly accepted by the other young artists, who became very fond of her. "I was everyone's pet," Georgia said, "which was kind of nice." Her new friends nicknamed her "Patsy" to go with her Irish last name.

Georgia's favorite class was advanced portrait painting. William Merritt Chase, a famous painter, taught the class. He was full of energy and style. He wore a top hat and a flower in his buttonhole. Chase taught his students to use aspects of all the great artists' styles, not to copy just one painter's technique.

He made his students create a new painting every single day. "We'd paint right over the old ones until the canvas got too thick," Georgia said later.

Patsy was having loads of fun. She loved the parties, the pranks, the dances, the boyfriends. Art students were constantly asking her to pose for them. The attention was flattering. And it also helped her earn a few needed dollars.

Everything seemed to be going right for Georgia. So why did she feel something was wrong? One day it became clear. She cut a class to sit for a portrait. The painter, a male classmate, teased her. He told her it didn't matter whether she went to class or not. It didn't really matter what she did. "You'll probably end up teaching painting in some girl's school," he said. "*I'm* going to be a great painter."

That was a shock! What had happened to the girl who had announced the very same thing a few years ago? What about giving everything up for art? Instead, she had chosen dancing and parties and fun, not to mention posing for other people's work.

That kind of life was keeping her from accomplishing her goal. "If I danced all night, I couldn't paint for three days," Georgia recalled. So she stopped. With the self-control she would show again and again, she rededicated her life to art.

About this time Georgia met someone just as dedicated to his art. His name was Alfred Stieglitz. His art was photography—something many artists and critics didn't consider "real" art. Stieglitz had a tiny gallery called 291, at 291 Fifth Avenue. He exhibited new, controversial works there, and he loved to argue about them.

Georgia and Alfred met on a snowy night in 1908. She and some other students had gone to 291 to see some drawings by the French sculptor Rodin. Many people said the drawings weren't very good. Some people even thought Rodin was playing a joke on Stieglitz.

"If I danced all night, I couldn't paint for three days."

The drawings didn't make much of an impression on Georgia. She found them "just little scribbles. They didn't look like anything I had been taught about drawing." But Stieglitz did make an impression on her, and not a very good one. He defended the Rodin drawings violently, which made Georgia very uncomfortable.

She finished her year at the League with great success. She hadn't yet developed her own artistic style. But she had brilliantly mastered all the techniques and use of materials she had been taught. Her still life of a dead rabbit and a copper pot won her a scholarship to a League summer art program at a lake in upstate New York.

A Turning Point

The summer of 1908 marked a real turning point in Georgia's artistic development. While at the lake, she kept trying to capture the pretty landscapes. But for some reason she felt blocked. She was frustrated. One evening at twilight she sat staring glumly at a marsh. "It all looked like I felt," she said later. "All damp and gloomy and wet and swampy."

Suddenly she knew what was missing in her work: *feelings.* How she felt affected how she saw and painted a scene.

Alfred Stieglitz, a photographer, ran a small gallery called 291. There, many new and exciting artists exhibited their work.

It was a great leap away from the formulas and composition techniques she had learned so well. Inspired by this new awareness, Georgia went on to paint a marsh picture that she thought was her best work of the summer.

She returned to Williamsburg for what she thought would be a short vacation before returning to the Art Students League. But by now her family had serious money troubles. No matter how deserving she was, there wasn't enough money to send Georgia back to school.

She tried to take it philosophically. She was concerned for her father, and she wanted to help. She wrote to a friend: "The wisest thing for [me] to do is to wake up …and see what [I] can do…. I am going to get busy and work regularly."

So once again, in the fall of 1908, Georgia boarded a train for Chicago. Once again she stayed with Aunt Ollie and Uncle Charles. But there were no more art classes. She got a job drawing products like household cleaners for newspaper ads.

While still in Chicago, Georgia got sick. She came down with the measles, which affected her eyesight, making work impossible. In 1909, she came home to Virginia.

Things at home had become worse. Her father's business was a disaster. Her mother had tuberculosis. She turned her mind to the job of helping her family. Her own plans had to be put on hold for awhile.

By the winter of 1910-1911, Georgia lost hope of ever returning to school. At the same time, she was unable to make a living from her art. Because women were discouraged from becoming artists, there were very few role models to inspire her. All of a sudden it seemed hopeless. There were just too many obstacles standing in the way of becoming an artist. She announced she was giving up painting.

Chapter 4

A New Direction

For months, Georgia didn't come near a paint brush. She really meant what she had said. But in the spring of 1911, Elizabeth Willis, Georgia's art teacher at Chatham, asked her to teach a class for six weeks. Georgia agreed. Teaching others art wasn't the same thing as painting herself. And she needed something to do.

Georgia, in 1915, at the age of 28.

She was a good teacher, and she found she liked teaching. She tried not to think of the comment the art student in New York had made to her about her winding up teaching art at a girls' school. Now here she was, doing exactly that. Still, teaching was a way to make money and be independent.

By 1912, Georgia found she couldn't stay completely away from painting after all. That summer she took some classes with a man named Alon Bement.

23

Bement made a big difference in Georgia's artistic progress. He thought a painting should be more than just a copy of an object. It should show the artist's thoughts and feelings. Instead of just painting a picture of a flower, an artist should also paint how the flower made her feel.

This idea reminded Georgia of what she had discovered at the lake when she painted the marsh. Bement was telling her to listen to her own instincts and emotions. Then she should express them in paintings. "Art could be a thing of your own," Georgia thought.

Alon Bement had given Georgia a great gift. She would paint again after all. And she would paint in her very own way. At least, that's what she would do someday. But right now she had to earn some money. At the end of the summer of 1912, she accepted another job teaching art—this time in Amarillo, Texas.

"Art could be a thing of your own," Georgia thought.

Wide Open Spaces

Georgia found a rough new world of rugged beauty in Texas. She also found a school so new it didn't have books yet. That didn't bother her. She used the natural world around her to teach her students.

An interior view of the 291 gallery.

Georgia took her students for long walks on the prairie. She showed them how to draw the tall weeds. They learned to draw lines on paper and divide the spaces into designs. She never asked them to copy pictures. Instead, they drew rocks, tumbleweeds—objects they saw around them. She wanted them to find beauty in the everyday world, as she did. She was a special kind of teacher. Her students knew this and responded to her.

When Georgia wasn't teaching she walked out into the vast, open plains. Texas reminded her of her girlhood dollhouse. But instead of little spaces to fill with her imagination, she had miles of sky and land. There were no walls to make her feel closed in. There were dazzling, dramatic sunsets. She fell in love with "the beauty of that wild world."

When the school year ended, she returned to Virginia. This time she was Alon Bement's assistant, not his student. For two years, she spent the school year teaching in Amarillo and the summer in Virginia. By the summer of 1914, she had grown into a confident professional woman.

Although she felt good about herself and what she was doing, she still did not have a teaching degree. She really needed more schooling, but that cost money. Once again, she had none. Then Aunt Ollie came to the rescue. She offered to pay for Georgia to go to Columbia Teachers' College in New York City.

Back to New York! Back to school! It was a dream come true. For the third time, in the fall of 1914, Georgia set out for school. But this time, at age 27, she knew what she wanted to do and how to get it.

New Rules for Art

Georgia found life in New York different than she remembered. People were excited about new ideas in art and music and politics. Art, particularly, was changing dramatically.

The change had begun some years before, in the late 1800s. That was when painters such as Édouard Manet, Claude Monet, and Edgar Degas began looking for a different way to paint. They thought that a picture of flowers in a vase painted in a studio was artificial and lifeless. Instead, they painted flowers in natural sunlight and shadows outside.

Their techniques were different, too. They used quick strokes of unblended color. From a distance, the strokes and colors flowed together to create an *impression* of a flower instead of an exact copy.

These artists were trying to capture the feeling of what they saw. That's why they were called impressionists. Many people couldn't accept impressionism. They were used to looking at exact copies of objects. They thought this new work was sloppy and lacked skill.

Alfred Stieglitz was one of the very few people who recognized that these artists and their new kind of art were avant-garde, meaning before its time. Their paintings were totally unlike anything that had been done before. Even today, work that is considered avant-garde often has difficulty being accepted and enjoyed.

Stieglitz's gallery, 291, was a showcase for avant-garde art. Stieglitz gave the American public its first look at the modern French

An early Stieglitz photo shows the backyard of Gallery 291.

painters Cézanne and Toulouse-Lautrec. Picasso, a Spanish artist, had his first solo show at 291. Hundreds of people came to 291 to look at and argue about the art.

Stieglitz showed photography, too—his own work and that of others. He worked endlessly to make people understand that an image taken by a camera could be art as much as a painting. Stieglitz was most famous for photographs of the city scenes around him. The photos captured the energy and emotion of New York City life in the early twentieth century, from the waves of arriving immigrants to the tall, new buildings called skyscrapers. Some critics have called Stieglitz's style "urban realism."

Georgia visited the exciting world of 291 often. It was a stimulating place for people who loved art. But Stieglitz frightened her. She thought he asked "such personal questions." When her friend Anita Pollitzer argued with him, Georgia would slip away.

Georgia worked very hard that year. When it was over, her teachers called her "one of the most talented art students we have ever had."

When she got home to Virginia, Georgia met Arthur Macmahon. He was a tall, handsome man from New York City who was teaching political science at the University of Virginia for the summer. Their friendship grew during the summer.

But using her typical self-control, Georgia resisted romance. She held onto her independent spirit and lifestyle. She wrote to her friend Anita Pollitzer: "Self-control is a wonderful thing—I think we must even keep ourselves from feeling too much—often—if we are going to keep sane and see with a clear, unprejudiced vision."

Despite her determination, her attraction to Arthur kept growing. Arthur went back to New York City in the fall. She did not have enough money to return to the city. Georgia channeled her thoughts and feelings about Arthur into her art work.

With Arthur gone and her teaching job over at the University of Virginia, Georgia had to look for another job to earn a living. She found one at a small school in South Carolina. She was not paid much, but she did have time for her own work. Over the Christmas holidays, she spent every minute she could on a series of drawings, using only charcoal and no colors.

For three weeks she poured out her feelings in curving lines and sharp forms. These weren't pictures of objects. The

"Self-control is a wonderful thing..."

shapes showed tension, emotion, energy. The drawings expressed how she felt about art, about herself, and about Arthur.

She rolled up the drawings and sent them to Anita Pollitzer in New York. Anita was the only person who might understand what she was trying to say. She begged Anita not to show them to anyone else.

When Anita unrolled them, she saw at once that they were special. "Here were charcoals, on the same paper all art students were using, saying something that had not yet been said," Anita recalled. Despite Georgia's wishes, she took the drawings to Alfred Stieglitz.

It was late on a Saturday afternoon. The gallery had closed for the day, and Stieglitz was tired. But he took the time to carefully examine the drawings. He saw something he had never seen before.

"At last!" he exclaimed. "A woman on paper!" He told Anita he wanted to show the drawings in his gallery. "They are the purest, finest, sincerest things that have entered 291 in a long while."

Chapter 5

Back to the Desert

Alfred Stieglitz meant what he said. The next spring, 1916, he hung ten of Georgia's charcoal drawings along with two other artist's work. He did not have her permission to do so. The swirly, billowy, abstract drawings caused a stir. Art critics and ordinary people said they showed a "woman's feelings"—strong feelings. In the early twentieth century, many people thought feelings like love and passion should not be discussed, let alone displayed for all the world to see.

Georgia herself was back in New York by this time, at work on her teaching degree. She could afford it because Anita Pollitzer's uncle was letting her stay in his house rent-free. Georgia knew Anita had shown Stieglitz the charcoals, but she didn't know the drawings were being exhibited.

A photographic portrait of Georgia in 1918, by Alfred Stieglitz.

One day another student innocently mentioned that there were drawings by a "Virginia O'Keeffe" at Stieglitz's gallery. Georgia was furious and embarrassed, even though she respected Stieglitz's opinion more than almost anyone else's. She had once told Anita: "I believe I would rather have Stieglitz like something—anything I had done—than anyone else I know of." Nevertheless, she was still angry. It was agony for her to show her work—this work, of all things! These drawings represented her most private emotions, especially her love for Arthur Macmahon. One of the drawings was titled "Maybe a Kiss ...." Now these feelings were hung on a wall for the world to see.

"She always wore black...black, black, black. And no frills of any kind."

She stormed down Fifth Avenue and confronted Stieglitz. She demanded he take down the drawings. He refused. He said she had no right to withhold such marvelous art from the world.

Georgia gave in. The drawings stayed up. This was the beginning of professional recognition for Georgia. Unfortunately, that spring was also a time of tragedy. On May 2, 1916, Ida O'Keeffe died of tuberculosis. Georgia left New York to be with her family in Virginia.

A Blue Period

It took Georgia many weeks after her mother's death before she wanted to do much of anything. When she started painting again, the paintings were all blue. She titled them simply: *Blue Lines, Blue I, Blue II, Blue III,* and so on.

Some looked Oriental, with simple shapes and lines. Others were full of plumes and puffs, similar to some of the charcoal drawings Stieglitz had shown.

All of the work was abstract, no real objects were painted. There were no fruit bowls, portraits, or landscapes. Georgia O'Keeffe was creating something new. She was showing her own style, her own artistic vision.

Georgia sent the watercolors to Stieglitz and went back to Texas. She had found a job in the tiny town of Canyon, teaching art at a small college.

The small town didn't know what to make of the new art teacher. They'd never met a woman like Georgia. "She always wore black," a student recalled. "Black, black, black. And no frills of any kind."

As she had done in Amarillo, Georgia she spent hours roaming the desert, bringing back natural objects for her students to paint. She found beauty everywhere—even in cattle bones. The stark, white bones looked pure and powerful to her. Many years later, those bones would become strong images in her own paintings.

The changing colors of the prairie and canyons thrilled and amazed Georgia. Depending on the time of day, the landscape was washed in purples, golds, greens, oranges, and scarlets. She moved out of her "blue" period and opened up her palette to all the gorgeous possibilities.

While she was in Texas, she wrote to both Arthur Macmahon and Alfred Stieglitz. She still cared for Arthur. But Stieglitz was an artist. There was more Georgia could share with Stieglitz—insights, feelings, experiences. She shared her work, too, sending him each watercolor as it was finished.

She was in a dilemma. She was 29 years old. Most women her age were wives and mothers. She wanted to have children herself. She had no family money, so she would either have to support herself teaching the rest of her life or marry someone who could support her.

The practical thing to do would be to get married. But there was her work. Could she be a wife and a mother and still devote herself to art? The passion to be a painter kept rising up and dwarfing any other alternatives. And Alfred Stieglitz was doing his best to encourage that passion.

In the spring of 1917, he gave Georgia her own show at 291. Hanging were the landscapes she had been painting in Texas, called the Palo Duro landscapes, along with watercolors from her Blue period. Georgia sold a painting for $400—her first sale ever—and boarded a train back East.

Hands of Georgia O'Keeffe by Alfred Stieglitz.

Mixed Reaction

She found mixed reaction to her work. One critic looked at Blue Lines in male/female terms. He saw the two lines as a man's and a woman's life, with the woman's veering off to the side while the man's continued growing straight up. This was the first analysis of O'Keeffe's work that focused on male/female characteristics and themes. It would not be the last.

Back in Texas, Georgia started another series called *Evening Star.* In these ten paintings, rich curls of red, orange, and pink swirl around a white-centered yellow star. Underneath, purples, greens, and blues show the mountains and desert.

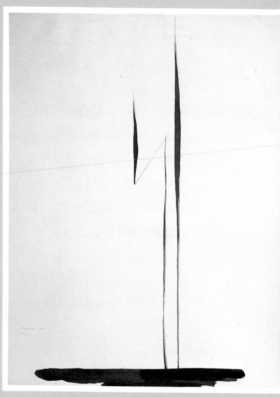

(Below)
Blue Number 2 was painted shortly after Georgia's mother died. All of her paintings of this period relied heavily on the color blue.

(Above)
Blue Lines, a watercolor on paper, caused a great stir in the art world when it was first shown in 1916. Some critics said it represented the two lines of life–a woman's and a man's.

(Opposite page)
Light Coming On the Plains II is another in the series of watercolors from Georgia's "Blue Period."

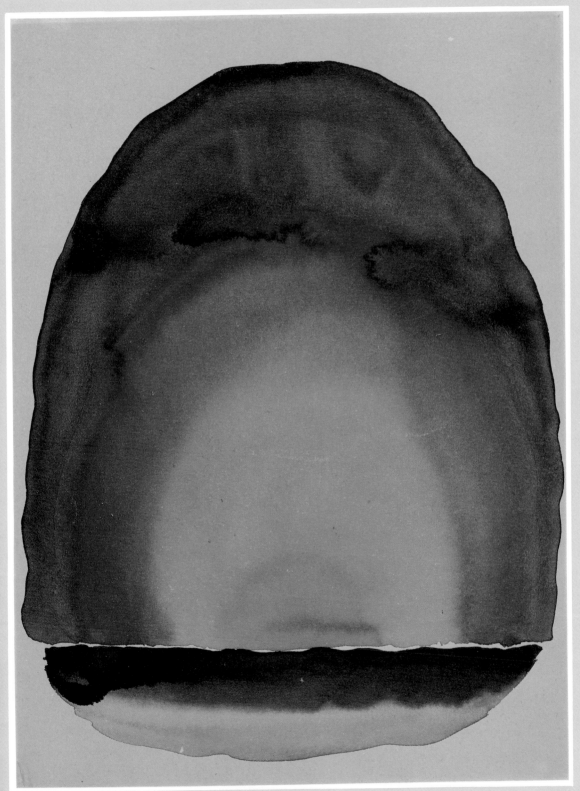

The paintings were daring and dramatic. Critics later called them "full of risks." The artist clearly revealed her changing moods and feelings. No two paintings were alike. Some were bright and bold. Others were hazy and subdued.

The *Evening Star* series would further O'Keeffe's reputation for using glorious color to make a dramatic statement. "Color is one of the great things in the world that makes life worth living to me," she said.

Georgia painted a lot that year, and Stieglitz was becoming more fascinated by her. They wrote often. At the same time, life started to sour for Georgia in the conservative little Texas town.

When the United States entered the war in Europe in 1917, Georgia took stands that set her apart from people in the town. This was World War I, and the United States was fighting against Germany. Many Americans were extremely anti-German, and patriotic feelings ran high.

Young men were encouraged to quit school and join the army. Georgia thought that this was a bad idea. She urged her male students to stay in school. Many people found this unpatriotic and unforgivable.

Georgia didn't like the war nor did she agree with what Germany was doing. But she also didn't like the bigotry she saw all around her. People hated anyone who was German or whose relatives had come from Germany. Georgia, on the other hand, did not think it was right that people were hated just because of their nationality. When she saw Christmas cards with hateful anti-German messages on them in a local shop, she asked the owner to remove them.

The whole town seemed to turn against her. Where she had felt free and happy, now she felt hated and shunned. "There is no one here I can talk to," she wrote in a letter. "It's like a bad dream."

Depressed and emotionally wounded, Georgia once again became physically ill—this time with the flu. There was an epidemic sweeping the country, and thousands had died that year. Georgia's friends outside Texas, especially Stieglitz, were concerned.

Meanwhile, Stieglitz was having his own problems. His marriage was unhappy, and 291 was being torn down. He felt on the fringes of the art world, where he had once been the center. Georgia was becoming more and more important to him.

Life in Canyon was finally unbearable for Georgia. She felt both physically and emotionally sick. She had to get away. Finally, Georgia escaped to a friend's nearby ranch.

Stieglitz sent another friend, Paul Strand, to bring Georgia back to New York. Still concerned about her health, he wanted her close to him.

Georgia wasn't sure. She loved the Southwest. There was so much to paint. She had done good work there.

And she was afraid—afraid of the way she was starting to feel about Stieglitz. What might happen to her—as an artist and as a woman—when they weren't separated by thousands of miles?

Still, there was nothing left for her in Texas. Paul Strand sent Stieglitz a telegram on June 8, 1918, saying he was bringing Georgia back.

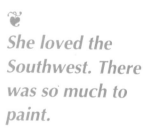

She loved the Southwest. There was so much to paint.

Chapter 6

A Career in Full Flower

When Georgia reached New York, she was tired and ill. Stieglitz brought her to his niece's apartment to rest for several weeks. At first, Stieglitz came to visit and talk about art, but his attraction to her quickly grew. She also could not control her feelings for him. She had once warned her good friend Anita Pollitzer that "love will eat you up and swallow you whole." But now Georgia was unable to heed her own warning. She was in love with Stieglitz.

Stieglitz's wife, Emmy, was a wealthy woman. Her money made his artistic work possible, but they had little in common. The only real connection they had was their daughter, Kitty. When Georgia re-entered his life, Stieglitz made the decision to leave Emmy and live with her. By the social standards of the early twentieth century, this was a very shocking thing to

Georgia O'Keeffe, 1935.

do. Georgia and Alfred, both blinded by love and happiness, ignored the comments of friends and family.

Alfred's family, however, was not upset with the breakup of his marriage. His mother, brothers, and sisters had known for many years that he was in an unhappy marriage. When Stieglitz brought Georgia to his family's summer home in Lake George, New York, she was welcomed with open arms.

Spending time with a large, noisy family was a jolt to Georgia. For many years she had been living alone or at boarding schools. Now she was in the middle of a family that shared every meal, every argument. Still, she was happy to be with the man she loved and, as always, to be painting. For the next ten years, the summer trip to Lake George was an annual event for them both.

Finally, Freedom to Paint

When autumn came they returned to New York City. Stieglitz arranged for an investor to loan Georgia money. Now she didn't have to teach. She could paint all day, every day. People were beginning to want to buy her work. But she found it hard to part with it. Each picture was special to her. When one was sold she grieved.

During the summer of 1923, Stieglitz opened a show. He advertised it this way:

> Alfred Stieglitz
> presents
> One Hundred Pictures
> Oils, Water-Colors,
> Pastels, & Drawings
> by
> Georgia O'Keeffe,
> American

Alfred Stieglitz with some of Georgia's paintings. He often gave lectures to art students on her work.

Thousands of people came to see the exhibit of Georgia's work. Some of the pictures were landscape paintings done at Lake George. There were also small, vibrantly colored pictures of flowers.

The art critics argued about what they saw. They were accustomed to paintings by male artists. This work by a woman was hard to put in a category. Did O'Keeffe paint like this because she was female? The question angered Georgia. She was annoyed when people labeled her a "woman artist." She felt she painted what she saw and how it made her feel, just as any artist did.

She was also upset when some artists said that the only reason anyone came to see her work was because she was Stieglitz's lover. This made her so furious she avoided talking with people.

Regardless of what people said about her work, she was very productive. For the next six years, Stieglitz had an annual show of her work.

A Huge Petunia

Georgia's work gradually became more abstract. The shapes in her paintings were stunning. She said even she didn't know where they came from. The colors became deeper and more intense, and she became bolder. A new series of flower paintings were startling. Some of them were so large they seemed to push against the edges of the canvas. Even Stieglitz was shocked when he saw her painting of a huge purple petunia. "Well, Georgia," he told her, "I don't know how you're going to get away with anything like that."

People were used to seeing pictures of flowers, but these pictures were different. Instead of painting a vase full of flowers, Georgia painted immense flower petals that seemed to put the viewer inside the blossom. "Most people in the city rush around so, they have no time to look at a flower. I want them to see it whether they want to or not," she explained.

The size of the flowers made people feel as if they had shrunk, like Alice in Wonderland, into a private world. People also saw her work as very sexual. There had never been paintings like this.

And the colors! At the time, most artists were painting in dark, somber colors—blacks, greys, browns. Georgia's paintings glowed: strong reds, velvety purples, and pure, gleaming white. She also tried to simplify the flower, to show its beauty in the clearest way possible.

Once again, Georgia O'Keeffe had given the art world something to think about. The problem was, no one could agree on what exactly that was. One critic insisted that she wanted people to feel "as if we humans were butterflies." Most of the art critics were men, and they found themselves deeply disturbed by the paintings. How could a woman seem to expose so much of herself, yet be so mysterious? Women reacted differently to the flowers. They came in large numbers and stood in silent wonder and appreciation.

"Most people in the city rush around so, they have no time to look at a flower. I want them to see it whether they want to or not."

(Above)
The Radiator Building–Night, New York is an oil painting done in 1927. Georgia was living and working in New York at the time.

(At right)
Corn Dark, I was painted in 1924. One can begin to see Georgia's fascination with the natural forms that became so important in her later work.

Black Iris III, painted in 1926, was one of Georgia's early flower paintings. She wanted to make people aware of the abstract shapes and colors of flowers.

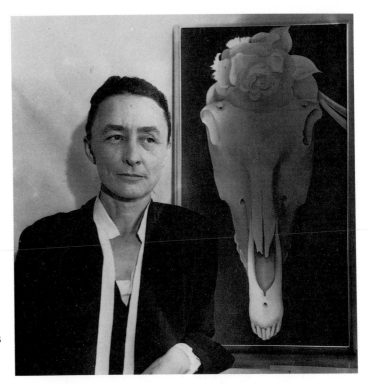

Georgia with one of her famous paintings. The bull's skull became her most well-known image.

Georgia's life as an artist was changing and so was her life with Stieglitz. When Emmy finally agreed to a divorce in 1924, Alfred and Georgia quietly married.

Georgia wanted to have a baby, but Stieglitz insisted he was too old to be a father again. He told Georgia that having children would make it too difficult for her to paint. She sadly let him have his way.

By 1928, their lives had slipped into a regular routine. Winters were spent in New York City, summers at Lake George surrounded by Stieglitz's family. It appeared pleasant on the surface, but Georgia was beginning to feel trapped.

Living with Stieglitz, Georgia found herself making compromises. She wanted to visit other places. He insisted on returning to Lake George every summer. He was nearly 65 years old and his health was fragile. Her love and concern for him conflicted with her need for new painting ideas. For years, Lake George had provided her with plenty of subjects to paint. Now she felt the dark green hills and thick pine trees were smothering her imagination.

In 1929, her annual show had only 35 paintings. She was 42 years old and feeling tired and frustrated. When a friend invited her along on a trip to Taos, New Mexico, she quickly accepted. Stieglitz was unhappy to see her go. As an artist, he knew she was searching for something. But he was afraid she wouldn't come home.

Call of the Southwest

Taos had attracted artists for many years. Painters loved the clear, thin air that made the colors so intense. Alone, surrounded by the kind of rugged open spaces she had always admired, Georgia felt that she could breathe again. "I don't know whether you know how important these days are for me, but I feel it so," she wrote to a friend in New York.

She felt much better when she returned to New York. But she quickly discovered a new problem. Stieglitz had a new assistant, Dorothy Norman. Georgia was soon aware of how important Dorothy had become to Stieglitz. He relied on her the same way he had relied on Georgia when they first met. The tension between husband and wife grew. The following summer Georgia returned to New Mexico.

Their relationship seemed to be coming apart. She was finding new friends and subjects to paint in New Mexico. In New York, Stieglitz had Dorothy to help run his gallery and fill his empty hours.

When Georgia returned to New York, she brought a barrel of sun-bleached animal bones and colorful fabric flowers. She was trying to capture some of the feeling of the Southwest and bring it to New York. After New Mexico, New York felt grey and closed in. Her paintings done during this time are dark and tight. She counted the days until she could go to New Mexico again.

By the end of 1932, Georgia was on the edge of emotional collapse. The strain of Stieglitz's relationship with Dorothy and her difficulty in finding a new painting direction was too much. Her world finally came crashing down.

Chapter 7

One with the Land

As had happened so often before, Georgia's body responded to her mental distress. She began having chest pains and blinding headaches. She went into a hospital, tired and depressed. It was one of the lowest points in her life, and she lashed out at others in anger and frustration. Unfortunately, she took her suffering out on her sister Catherine who was also a painter. When Catherine's show in New York opened, many of the paintings shown were giant-sized flowers, like Georgia's. In the past, Georgia had encouraged Catherine. Now she wrote her sister a furious letter from the hospital, threatening to tear all her paintings to pieces. Catherine never painted again.

For the next six months Georgia was a semi-invalid. Released from the hospital in

Georgia, shortly after becoming a member of the Academy of Arts and Letters, an honor society for artists.

51

"She is not painting," he wrote someone. "May never paint again."

March, she spent time resting in Lake George and in Bermuda. Meanwhile, Alfred Stieglitz was worried.

"She is not painting," he wrote someone. "May never paint again."

Georgia did eventually recover. But something had changed within her. She had an even deeper need for being alone, for her own space, than ever before. She knew she could find the solitude and artistic freedom she needed only in her beloved New Mexico. So she went back, leaving Stieglitz in New York.

Back to the Source

The dry desert outside once again turned on a tap inside Georgia. She would drive deep into the hills and canyons and paint. When it got too hot she would slip under her car and rest till it was cooler. At night she'd climb up on the flat, tiled roof of her ranch house and lie there watching the starry sky. (She would later paint a stunning picture called "Ladder to the Moon," showing a ladder floating in space, pointing up to a brilliant moon.)

She painted red and grey hills and cliffs that seemed to be, as she said, "reaching out to the sky." She painted stones and more flowers and, more and more, animal bones bleached in the desert sun. From this period, skulls, antlers, and pelvic bones of cattle and antelope became almost as much her trademark as her enormous flowers.

Sometimes Georgia mixed the two, adding flowers to the bone arrangements for the startling effect. Several paintings showed circles of sky through pelvic bones. Her work was mostly abstract. People admired it for the powerful shapes, detailed shading, and splashes of brilliant color.

Georgia O'Keeffe was in full swing again as an artist. In fact, she was famous now, with a thousand people a week viewing her work at Stieglitz's gallery, An American Place. She was also earning a good living. Her paintings were selling for at least $5,000 apiece for some time. (When she died, her estate would be worth $50 million.)

Her husband's relationship with Dorothy Norman had quieted, and Georgia and Stieglitz were still very devoted to each other. Despite the devotion, though, they only lived together six months out of the year. The rest of the time he was in New York or Lake George while she lived her rugged, primitive life in New Mexico. Georgia's house was miles out of town and

(*Opposite, top*)
A view of the mountains near Abiquiu, New Mexico where Georgia owned a ranch. This was painted in 1930.

(*Opposite, below*)
This large oil painting, titled *From the Faraway Nearby*, was painted in 1937. Again, the cattle skull and the mountains of New Mexico are used.

(*Top, this page*)
This painting, one of a series inspired by cloud formations, is titled, *Sky Above Clouds IV*. It was painted in 1965 and records the artist's impressions after flying home to New Mexico from an around-the-world trip.

(*At left*)
Ladder to the Moon is a playful, fantasy painting based on Georgia's endless fascination with the sky of the Southwest.

A ladder leaning against the wall of Georgia's house was the inspiration for *Ladder to the Moon* (see page 55).

had no electricity or running water. Her elderly, sickly husband could not have stayed there even if they both had wanted him to.

Alfred and Georgia knew their situation was not ideal, but it was the best compromise they could make. Georgia would never let her art take second place to anything or anyone, even Stieglitz. The price was too high: It was her whole soul and sense of self-esteem. Art had the number one position in her life, and it would remain there always.

A Last Goodbye

In 1946, while working outdoors on a painting, Georgia got a message that Alfred had collapsed in his gallery. By the time she reached New York, he was in a coma. He died a few days later, at the age of eighty-two.

After Alfred's funeral, Georgia took his ashes to Lake George, where she buried them at the edge of the water. "I put him where he could hear the Lake," she wrote. Then she set about cataloging and organizing his huge collection of art, photographs, and letters. Several museums and two universities, Yale and Fisk, received everything valuable.

This work took her three years. Finally, in 1949, she moved back to New Mexico for good.

Georgia spent the next two decades traveling, entertaining guests, becoming involved in her community, and, of course, painting. With Alfred's death, she no longer had a connection to New York and the art circles there. She was also no longer tied to another person. Now she was free to concentrate on herself on her beloved Southwest desert.

A few years before, she had bought a run-down ranch near Abiquiu, New Mexico. She restored the buildings and made this her home. At first, the mostly Hispanic villagers were suspicious of the Anglo woman, but in time they came to accept her. Since her paintings continued to sell at good prices, she had money, and she was generous with it. She had hired local people to work on her house, and when the place was livable, she hired more people to help her run it. She even split up the household duties so she could hire as many people as possible.

She saw needs in the community and did everything she could to meet them. She put up money to build a gym so the young people could have a place to play. She paid

Georgia, 1956, in a portrait by Canadian photographer Yousef Karsh.

for a clean drinking water system for the town. She helped finance a new elementary school. She gave children money to go the movies and did much more than that for some teen-agers: she actually paid their college tuition.

Georgia entertained often at her ranch, usually her sisters and their children and grandchildren or close friends such as Anita Pollitzer. She traveled outside the United States for the first time in her life, going to Europe in 1953 and Peru in 1956. In 1959, she went around the world.

As always, she kept working. And she kept looking for new ways to paint, new perspectives. During her travels—especially her flights around the world—she became interested in aerial views. She began a series called *Rivers Seen From Air.* Although critics didn't find them as powerful as her other work, the paintings reflect the growing importance of sky in her work during these later years.

One of the loveliest from this series is called *It Was Yellow and Pink,* showing rivers looking like graceful yellow trees branching out on a pink prairie. Other paintings from this period also feature the sky: *From the Plains I and III, Ladder to the Moon.*

By 1965, the public had almost forgotten about Georgia O'Keeffe. She had lived close to a hermit's life in New Mexico, far removed from the inner circles of the American art world. She was 78 years old. But she wasn't ready to stop yet.

While flying back to New Mexico one day she became fascinated by the way the sky looked. It was, she remembered, "the most beautiful solid white. It looked so secure that I thought I could walk right out on it to the horizon if the door opened. The sky beyond was a light clear blue. It was so wonderful that I couldn't wait to be home to paint it."

That vision turned into a breathtaking word called *Sky Above Clouds IV.* It was a long, horizontal painting of blue sky and white oval-shaped clouds, rows and rows of them. What made this painting unbeliev-able was its size. It was more than 20 feet wide—truly as big as a house.

Georgia's talent and genius hadn't di-minished. But her body was feeling the effects of old age. One day in 1971 she realized she had lost some of her sight. How could she be partially blind—and still be an artist? She soon sank into a deep depression.

"The sky beyond was a light clear blue. It was so wonderful that I couldn't wait to be home to paint it."

Georgia with Alexander Calder, the American sculptor best known for his "moving sculptures," called mobiles.

Georgia with young potter, Juan Hamilton, in 1979.

Then a young man named Juan Hamilton stopped by her house looking for a job. He ended up being Georgia's companion. Juan was a potter. He taught Georgia to make hand-thrown pots—creating art with hands instead of eyes. He encouraged her to try and paint again. Georgia was grateful and equally supportive. She even persuaded some dealers to display his pots with her paintings.

Many people say Juan took advantage of an old woman for personal gain. But one thing is sure: Georgia's last years were productive. If Juan —or someone like him—hadn't come along, that might not have been the case.

Georgia O'Keeffe received many awards during her life. But since she spent much of her time fighting for artistic and personal freedom, it's especially fitting that she was awarded the Medal of Freedom in 1979.

Several years later, too ill to stay on her ranch, she moved to Santa Fe. She died in 1986 at the age of 98. Her work is testimony to an artistic genius who lived every day of her life with passion and courage.

Glossary

Explaining New Words

abstract art Paintings that are not copies of objects but use shapes or colors to show artists' interpretation of objects. Viewers can have different ideas about what these paintings mean.

art critics People whose job is expressing their opinions about painters and works of art.

avant-garde A French expression meaning "first," used to describe new paintings, music, or other art that is very different from what's come before.

canvas A piece of cloth backed or framed as a surface for painting.

composition The way the elements or items in a painting or photograph are arranged together.

easel The frame that supports an artist's canvas.

essence Those important qualities that give a person, idea, or object an identity that is different from all others.

fine art Paintings, sculpture, and other types of artwork created to be enjoyed for their beauty rather than to be used in more practical ways.

gallery A room or building where artwork is displayed, for public viewing.

impressionism A type of art that began in the 1800s in which paintings give an impression of a scene or object instead of a realistic picture. Impressionistic works look looser and less precise than more "traditional" art. They often use patterns of light, shadow, and color to create their effect. **61**

instinct An unexplained feeling or sense about something that comes not from thinking but from somewhere deep within you.

landscape A painting or drawing of land, mountains, or other outdoor scenery.

palette A flat surface used by a painter to mix color, traditionally oblong with a hole for the thumb.

scale The relationship (smaller or larger) of an object to its representation in a drawing or painting.

sit In artistic terms, to pose for a portrait.

studio A room or building where an artist works.

urban realism Photographs or paintings that realistically show the details of life in a city.

For Further Reading

Callaway, Nicholas, ed. *One Hundred Flowers.* New York: Alfred A. Knopf, 1989.

Gherman, Beverly. *Georgia O'Keeffe: The "Wideness and Wonder" of Her World.* New York: Atheneum, 1986.

Haskell, Barbara (essay). *Georgia O'Keeffe: Works on Paper.* Santa Fe: Museum of New Mexico Press, 1985.

Lisle, Laurie. *Portrait of an Artist: A Biography of Georgia O'Keeffe.* New York: Seaview, 1980.

O'Keeffe, Georgia. *Georgia O'Keeffe.* New York: Penguin Books, 1976.

Pollitzer, Anita. *A Woman on Paper.* New York: Touchstone/Simon & Schuster, 1988.

Robinson, Roxana. *Georgia O'Keeffe: A Life.* New York: Harper & Row, 1989.

Index

Photo credits:

Page 1, Malcolm Varon, 1977; p. 4: The State Historical Society of Wisconsin; pps. 6, 7, 8, 11: Courtesy of Catherine Krueger; pps. 13, 16, 41, 43: The Bettmann Archive; p. 15: Painting by Eugene Speicher, Courtesy of The Art Students League of N.Y.; p. 21: 1907, The Metropolitan Museum of Art, The Alfred Stieglitz Collection, 1955; p. 23: Holsinger Studio Collection, Special Collection Department, Manuscripts Division, University of Virginia Library; p. 25: Miriam and Ira D. Wallach Division of Art, Prints and Photographs, The N.Y. Public Library, Astor, Lenox and Tilden Foundations; p. 28: Alfred Stieglitz, From the Window of "291", 1915, The Alfred Stieglitz Collection, 1949, 1990, The Art Institute of Chicago, all rights reserved; p. 31: The Metropolitan Museum of Art, Gift of David A. Schulte; p. 35: The Metropolitan Museum of Art, Gift of Mrs. Rebecca S. Strand, 1928, The Metropolitan Museum of Art; p. 36, bottom-left: 1916, The Brooklyn Museum; p. 36, top-right: The Metropolitan Museum of Art, The Alfred Stieglitz Collection, 1969, photo by Malcolm Varon; p. 37: The Amon Carter Museum; p. 46, left: The Alfred Stieglitz Collection, The Carl Van Vecten Gallery of Fine Arts, Fisk University; p. 46 right: The Metropolitan Museum of Art, the Alfred Stieglitz Collection, 1950, photo by Malcolm Varon; p. 47: The Metropolitan Museum of Art, The Alfred Stieglitz Collection, 1969; pps. 48, 51, 59: UPI/Bettmann Newsphotos; p. 54, top: The Metropolitan Museum of Art, The Alfred Stieglitz Collection, 1963, photo by Malcolm Varon; p. 54, bottom: The Metropolitan Museum of Art, The Alfred Stieglitz Collection, 1959; p. 55, top: (detail) Restricted Gift of Paul and Gabriella Rosenbaum Foundation, and gift of Georgia O'Keeffe, 1990, The Art Institute of Chicago, all rights reserved; pps. 55, bottom, 56: Malcolm Varon, 1990; p. 58: Yousef Karsh/Woodfin Camp; p. 60: Dan Budnik/Woodfin Camp.